Roller Coasters

Precious McKenzie

Educational Media

rourkeeducationalmedia.com

Scan for Related Titles
and Teacher Resources

Teaching Focus Summarizing:

Summarizing requires students to determine what is important in what they are reading and to put it into their own words. Instruction in summarizing helps students:

- Identify or generate main ideas
- Connect the main or central ideas
- Eliminate unnecessary information
- Remember what they read

Before Reading:

Building Academic Vocabulary and Background Knowledge

Before reading a book, it is important to set the stage for your child or student by using pre-reading strategies. This will help them develop their vocabulary, increase their reading comprehension, and make connections across the curriculum.

1. *Read the title and look at the cover. Let's make predictions about what this book will be about.*
2. *Take a picture walk by talking about the pictures/photographs in the book. Implant the vocabulary as you take the picture walk. Be sure to talk about the text features such as headings, the Table of Contents, glossary, bolded words, captions, charts/diagrams, or index.*
3. *Have students read the first page of text with you then have students read the remaining text.*
4. *Strategy Talk – use to assist students while reading.*
   - *Get your mouth ready*
   - *Look at the picture*
   - *Think…does it make sense*
   - *Think…does it look right*
   - *Think…does it sound right*
   - *Chunk it – by looking for a part you know*
5. *Read it again.*
6. *After reading the book, complete the activities below.*

Content Area Vocabulary
Use glossary words in a sentence.

forces
friction
gravity
momentum
motorized
railway

After Reading:

Comprehension and Extension Activity

After reading the book, work on the following questions with your child or students in order to check their level of reading comprehension and content mastery.

1. *What keeps you from falling out of your seat when riding a roller coaster? (Inferring)*
2. *What do roller coasters use to whip the cars around the track? (Asking questions)*
3. *How many sets of wheels does a roller coaster have? (Text to self connection)*
4. *What kind of technology did inventors use to create new roller coasters? (Summarize)*

Extension Activity

Roller coasters are a favorite at every amusement park. You may not be able to ride one often, but you can make your own! Go to this website http://discoverykids.com/games/build-a-coaster/, and have an adult help you by clicking and dragging the icons onto the track to engineer and design your own thrill ride!

Table of Contents

Early Scream Rides

Do you like thrill rides? Have you ever been on a roller coaster?

④

The **forces of gravity** that affect the roller coaster's movement also affect riders' bodies. The weightless feeling at the top of a loop is gravity pulling you down while inertia pushes you up!

Roller coasters were invented in Russia 300 years ago.

Early roller coasters were sledges on icy and snowy slopes.

As technology changed, so did roller coasters. Inventors used **railway** technology to create new roller coasters.

Ron Toomer, a famous roller coaster designer, suffered from motion sickness. He rarely rode any of his thrilling inventions.

9

Like trains, roller coasters have cars, wheels, and a track.

Roller coasters are tested regularly by engineers. They look for loose bolts, rust, oil, and other things that could cause problems with the coaster's operation.

wheels

car

track

Roller coaster cars have three sets of wheels. Road wheels ride on top of the track. Upstop wheels are underneath the track. Guide wheels keep the cars from leaving the track sideways.

road wheels

guide wheels

upstop wheels

Faster!

Roller coasters use gravity and **momentum** to whip the cars around the track.

A **motorized** chain lift carries the cars to the top of the highest hill. The chain looks like a large bicycle chain.

At the top of the hill, gravity takes over as the cars speed down the hill.

gravity

Most roller coasters don't have engines. They operate by converting potential energy at the top of a hill into kinetic energy, which is the type of energy created once the coaster goes downhill.

Thanks to gravity, coasters can reach downhill speeds close to 70 miles (112 kilometers) per hour.

When cars go through loops, forces act on your body so you don't fall out.

force

The turns and curves on the track slow the cars and reduce the force.

Air resistance, **friction**, and brakes slow down and stop the coaster.

People must be a certain height to ride some roller coasters. This is because the safety restraints won't work for someone who is too small or too large.

choose Your RiDe

Steel roller coasters are higher and faster than wooden coasters.

Wooden coasters have more wobble. Whichever you choose, you'll have a screaming ride!

Photo Glossary

 **forces** (FORS-uhss): Forces are actions that change the movement or shape of an object. Gravity is an example of a force.

 **friction** (FRICK-shuhn): Friction is a force that slows down objects as they rub against one another.

 **gravity** (GRAV-uh-tee): This is the force that pulls objects toward Earth. Gravity is what keeps people and objects from floating into space.

momentum (moh-MEN-tuhm): Momentum is the force or speed that an object has when it is in motion.

motorized (MOH-tur-EYEZD): A machine that has a motor, which gives it power, is a motorized machine.

railway (RAYL-way): A railroad or the tracks for a train is called a railway.

InDex

WeBsites to Visit

www.kidzworld.com/article/4633-how-roller-coasters-work

http://pbskids.org/dragonflytv/show/rollercoasters.html

http://wonderopolis.org/wonder/how-do-roller-coasters-work

ABout the Author

Precious McKenzie lives in Montana with her husband and three children. But she was born in the Roller Coaster Capital of the United States—Sandusky, Ohio!

Meet The Author!
www.meetREMauthors.com

© 2017 Rourke Educational Media

www.rourkeeducationalmedia.com

PHOTO CREDITS: Cover © bukharova; Title Page © Pro-Syanov; Page 4 © Philartphace; Page 6 © Delfinkina; Page 7 © Chronicle/Alamy Stock Photo; Page 8 © George-Standen; Page 10 © Yana Bukharova && Denis Bukharova; Page 11 © Wikipedia; Page 12 © DIGIcal; Page 13 © MyImages-Micha; Page 14 © MarkP; Page 16 © SUNchese; Page 17 © Skyhobo; Page 18 © illusob; Page 20 © Photawa; Page 12 © tomh1000

Edited by: Keli Sipperley
Cover and interior design by: Jen Thomas

Library of Congress PCN Data

Roller Coasters / Precious McKenzie
(How It Works)
ISBN 978-1-68191-684-2 (hard cover)(alk. paper)
ISBN 978-1-68191-785-6 (soft cover)
ISBN 978-1-68191-884-6 (e-Book)
Library of Congress Control Number: 2016932560

Printed in the United States of America, North Mankato, Minnesota

Also Available as: